COUNTRY LOVE

vs.

CITY FLIRTATION.

INVIO

COUNTRY LOVE

vs.

CITY FLIRTATION;

OR,

TEN CHAPTERS FROM THE STORY OF A LIFE.

Reduced to Rhyme for convenience sake, by

.H. T. SPERRY,

WITH ILLUSTRATIONS BY

AUGUSTUS HOPPIN.

NEW YORK:
Carleton, Publisher, 413 *Broadway.*
MDCCCLXV.

THE N. Y. PRINTING COMPANY,
NOS. 34, 36, 38 & 40 ANN ST.
AND 102 & 105 NASSAU STREET,
NEW YORK.

TO

B. P. SHILLABER, Esq.,

(WITH MRS. PARTINGTON'S PERMISSION,)

THESE LEISURE MOMENT RHYMINGS,
IN THE HOPE THAT HE WILL BE PLEASED
WITH A PORTION OF THEM AT LEAST,
ARE RESPECTFULLY INSCRIBED

BY HIS FRIEND,

"INVIO."

Hartford, October, 1865.

List of Illustrations
Engraved By
Bobbett and Hooper

LIST OF ILLUSTRATIONS.

COUNTRY LOVE

vs.

CITY FLIRTATION.

I.

HOPE AND AMBITION.

Down where the wooden nutmegs grow,
Some ten or a dozen years or so,
Ago,
At the close of a day laconical,
In the latest season of gathering sheaves,

Of golden noons and glorious eves,
And the downward flight of forest leaves
  Begins this truthful chronicle:
A lonesome traveler might have been seen,
On the turnpike road near the village green,
In a grotesque suit of ultra-marine
  And a hat broad-brimmed and conical,
Awkwardly perched in a family cart—
  The very antiquest kind
Of an umbrella arching o'er him,
  A long black trunk behind
And a short white pony before him,
That ambles on with a jerk and a start,
As though it were taking an active part
  In a piece of German machinery.
His face, a mild picture of calm content,
Speaks, in each smile and lineament,
Of a noble heart and a firm intent,
Though his eyes on the turning wheels are bent

And not on the beautiful scenery.
Young in years, with a powerful arm,
And a robust form that would please and charm
The sculpture-critics, gained on the farm,
And not by a fashionable tailor's trick,
Strong in sinew and lithe of limb,
Few in fact can compare with him,
Though they call him only a specimen brick
Of the wooden nutmeg nation.
The pony jogs on with its rustic load,
Down the winding turns of the silent road.
Now under the swaying hemlock boughs,
Draped with the scented vines,
Round Adder-hill, where the cattle browse,
Then through the gloomy pines,
And reaches the railroad station,
Where the white hair'd Parson, with wondering
eyes,
Looks over his specs, in a queer surprise,

On beholding our hero, Reuben Grey,
And asks him why he is going away.

"Going," he says, in a husky tone,
"Going to try the great world alone—
To gain for myself a famous name,
With funded gold and a crown of fame
In the hum of the city, where toil and strife
Are the same at the ebb and flow of life;
Going away from the loved and the good
And the silent grave in the solemn wood,
The spring's sweet smiles and the autumn sheaves,
The blushing rose and crimsoning leaves,
And the twittering swallows under the eaves,
The springing grass and the brilliant dyes
That dawn and die in the sunset skies,
The cattle meek, with their great brown eyes,
And the drowsy noons and the droning bees,
The bobolink's song and the burdened breeze

OR THE ENG NE
THE BELL RINGS
Augs. Hoppin

That drifts from the blossoming orchard trees;
Going away from the meadow and brook,
The forest paths and the well-known nook
Where Percy sat with a closéd book,
And her promise gave in blesséd words,
Sweeter than ever the song of birds;
From the village church and the ancient mill,
The shadowy grave-yard dank and still,
And the sorrowful call of the whip-poor-will,
Things that I love and treasure still;
But the saddest of all, alas! to me,
Is to leave the homestead and Percy Lee;
For wearisome years must come and go
Ere I can forge, with a final blow,
The crown that my life and longing brain
Must call their own when we meet again;
  I shall toil and strive till I fully earn
    My prize in the race of life,
  Then from my wanderings I shall return
    And Percy will be a wife."

The Parson looks sad, for many an one
Has failed when the race was nearly run,
Despair'd ere the labor was half begun,
Or died when the work was almost done;
He has witnessed such things in his life and day,
But refrains from any prediction,
And bowing his head in a reverent way
Gives Reuben a calm benediction.

II.

SEEING THE WORLD.

With a thrilling shriek of terror and might,
    Into the darkness, into the night,
The booming train, with the speed of the wind,
    Flashes away like a gleam of light,
And the loving and loved are far behind.
    Now it rumbles among the trembling hills,
      And teārs through the mountain pass,
    "And many a league of shadow" that lies
      On the black and fear'd morass,
        Like a demon toward its doom!
    Then, past groaning and jarring mills,

With luminous panes, like fiendish eyes
    Peering into the gloom.
On through the forest bathed in perfume,
  From solemn and odorous pines,
Dark villages, draped in the hush of the tomb,
  And streets where the gas-light shines.

But our hero thinks not of these vanishing sights
    Of the night or the coming day,
For he goes, with his thoughts, in swallow flights,
To the scenes of home and their dear delights,
    Into mem'ries fading away.

Wearied at last, and heart and brain
Like lead with the weight of a nameless pain,
    Though hope and aspiration
Abide with him still, he dreamlessly sleeps,
While the rushing train on its fierce way keeps,
    And nears its destination.

The night and the journey are over and past,
And the turbulent city is gained at last,
Then with the old life Reuben shakes hands
And thinking the new over, finally stands
In the rushing and clamorous human tide,
Where the good and the bad, the grave and the gay,
Proud Dives and meek Lazarus, side by side,
Eternally drift through the bright Broadway;
Devotees of fashion, in feathers and paint,
Despising each other though gayly they meet;
And frail flaunting creatures, whose presence would taint
The homes of the men they smilingly greet;
And sad-faced children, with woful want
Photographed in their pleading eyes;
And imbecile women, pale and gaunt,
Thinking of death as a glorious prize;
Crowds of mercenary merchants and men.

With aberratic and troubled looks ;
And authors, whose features speak of the pen
As mousing critics will of their books ;
And flocks of merry and frolicksome girls,
With argent brows and innocent eyes,
And ripening lips and bewildering curls,
For which (in verses) the Poet dies ;
Squads of beggars, in squalor and rags,
Stamped with anguish and sorrow and crime,
Of human life the settlings and fags,
With no bright hopes of a better time ;
And vulgar plebeians, aping the Ton,
And Potiphar promenaders,
Plumed like the orient-bird,
All mingling together, and sweeping on
In a strange fantastic herd
Of grotesque masqueraders,
Confusing our hero ; alas ! for him,
In the crowded streets he is still alone,

Augs Hoppin

His heart throbs faint and his hopes grow dim,
  And he longs for a well-remembered tone,
    And the old familiar faces,
And tranquil hours his life hath known
    In the pleasant woodland places.

III.

INCONSTANCY.

Two changing years have swiftly glided by,
And Reuben, from his aspirations high
Of bold emprise and bright imaginings,
Hath fallen earthward on ignoble wings.
His hopes are plumed for starward flights no
more—
They merely circle round a Broadway store!
His high ambition now to see his name
Emblazoned—the antipodes of fame—
Upon a gilded sign above the door.
The glad, sweet music of his childhood years

Is silence-buried ; he only hears,
With anxious ears, the sharp metallic chimes
Of future dollars grown from present dimes.

His home-made garb is laid aside,
And he is completely transmogrified
Into a mincing New York clerk,
Learning to talk and smile and smirk
    In the very genteelest fashion ;
His work-brown'd hands are becoming white,
  And his features are growing fair,
And he sports a glass to aid his sight,
And kids and boots decidedly tight,
  With stylish things the young men wear,
    In order to properly dash on ;
Is dressed a-la-mode, and all perfumed
Like a massive bouquet freshly bloomed
  In the sweltering hot-house air,
And prides himself on his talk and face,

And displays new silks and French point lace,
With such a display of snobbish grace
  As to make his employers stare.

O, very unique are his elegant ways,
Attracting the notice and winning the praise
Of fashionable girls, and the ardent gaze
  Of many magnificent ladies ;
And very delectable 'tis, they say,
To perambulate, as the bon-ton may,
On the broadcloth side of the bright Broadway,
When palatial bazaars on opening day
Make a gorgeous splurge and a grand display
  Of goods from Paris or Cadiz,
To stop on a ravishing trading visit
And see him perform the role of exquisite
Over the counter of "Cheatum & Fibit,"
  Where "gammon" part of the trade is.
But comical 'tis to witness the pique,

Revealed by his motions and blushing cheek,
When rough country cousins earnestly seek
For him in the crowd,
And, with voices loud,
Tell him how all the people "tu hum"
Wonder and ask why he doesn't come
Down to the village and stay a spell;
How Brindle sickened and then got well,
When the pork was killed, how much it weighed,
How the barn, where he had worked and played,
Was fired, one desolate, windy night,
And what a grief and terrible fright
His father and mother and all were in;
How his sister was looking pale and thin;
Who had been buried, and how Will Lee
Brought home a young wife from Italy,
And filled a very respectable niche
In their best society;
And with what anxiety

And perfect propriety
Percy was waiting for him to grow rich,—
And many an uncouth thing beside,
Of home-brewed gossip and village news,
That wounds his shallow and pompous pride,
Reddens his face and gives him the blues;
For he's quite refined and doesn't choose
To have his companions think or know
He sprouted from anything so low
As the rustic sphere of a farmer's boy,
'Though 'twas glorified by a sinless joy,
And pure and free from the world's alloy.

"Marry come up," there is something here,
Something to think of, something to fear,
For Reuben forgets the vows of his youth,
And floats and drifts from the shores of truth,
Into the eddies of frivolous life,
Dreaming (alas! it is true and strange,

A young man's love is the first to change),
  Of an avenue palace, a wealthy wife,
      And a blazoned and princely station
  'Mong the million-a-year's, whose wearying strife
    Terminates and is gravely ended—
      Sad loss to a worshiping nation!—
    With a funeral grand and splendid,
      Or a very intense sensation,
    By shame and dishonor attended,
(Increased by Wall street Bulls and Bears,
Dreaded by friends and loving heirs,
And feared by wolves in banking lairs,)
    Caused by the curseful word "SUSPENDED."

Over village and city with noiseless tread,
  Years march on, as the Epic bard,
In pastoral legend, hath quaintly said,
To the unknown land, where the peaceful dead
  Take them under their solemn guard.

Through the busy hum of street and mart
Our hero moves with a burdened heart,
Burdened and worn with a prayer of gain
And a longing wish to rise and reign,
A Crœsus proud, o'er a wide domain!
Stoical still, as the long months wane,
To promises made in that blest time,
When his heart was pure, and hope sublime
Pictured to him a radiant crown
And an earnest life of high renown;
But pictured only and quick to fade,
Like mirage over an alpine glade,
Or asphodels in the forest shade,
Were the promises his young heart made.

He forgets, alas! his manly ruth,
His plighted constancy and truth,
Though conscience with remorseless tooth
Stings in a manner fearful,

Whenever the image of Percy Lee
Flits through the chambers of memory
Like a ghost that appals his soul to see,
  In its aspect sad and tearful.

But conscience must suspend its work
In the breast of *such* an ambitious clerk,
And should it ever presume to lurk
  Anywhere in his spirit's niches,
It must at once be ordered out;
At best 'tis only a country lout,
That isn't genteel to have about
  In the race for honor or riches.

At first the weekly mail bore down
To the dear old fashioned country town
  A letter to Percy Lee,
Full of professions marked and "loud;"
"His heart was sad 'mid the rushing crowd,

And his thoughts to her would flee;
'Mong all the ladies fair and proud
None were so fair as she!"
The same old story of mild deceit
That lying lips will still repeat
So long as time shall be.

And Percy believed it every word—
Her heart to its inmost depths was stirred,
And she sang her joy like a gladsome bird,
That made all happy its notes who heard.
But lighter far than a floating feather
The promises made by fickle men!
I grieve the scandalous fact to pen,
But his letters came only now and then,
And then stopped altogether;
On wings of gossip the story flew,
Till every one in the village knew
Its pros and cons, and it straightway grew,

On a very few recitals,
To as woful a tale as ever was told;
How Percy was fading—growing old;
And Reuben, while coining heaps of gold,
Was getting outrageously bad and bold,
And many opprobrious titles.

The village quidnuncs, wise and grave,
A version new of the matter gave
Whenever they came together;
Called him a snobbish cityfied scamp,
While others said,
With a toss of the head,
'Twas plain to see
For Percy Lee
He didn't care a postage stamp
In the glow of his summer weather.

IV.

WEARY WITH WAITING.

'Neath the greenery or under the snows
Nestles still, in its quiet respose,
The farm-house olden where Percy Lee
Waits with a weariless constancy,
Through heavy months and lingering years
And woful vigils of prayer and tears,
For golden fruitage of that dear hope,
Which hath been her life's bright horoscope
Since the darkened day the loved one went
Into the world with a great intent.

Sadly, alas! have the years of change
Marked her being, and tender and strange,
As the thrilling light that ever lies
In a loving woman's dreamful eyes,
Are the flitting smiles that sweetly trace
Her dearest thoughts on her pensive face;
And coldly tranquil and debonair,
Like a bright creation pure and fair,
A vision born of a poet's theme,
Or a shadowy form in a fitful dream,
Through all the forest and village ways,
From the quiet house to the murmuring stream,
She goes and comes, with her yearning gaze
Reaching beyond the desolate days,
To that glad time when a fond embrace,
The light of a well remembered face,
A loving voice and a trustful vow,
Shall lift the gloom that is brooding now
O'er her shrouded love and joyless life,

And quell the terrible inner strife
Of full-flushed hopes and skeleton fears,
Presaging with doubts the coming years.

Still Percy waits, and the days go by,
Dimming the light of her lustrous eye,
Changing the grace of her beautiful head,
The musical fall of her airy tread,
And her voice's low and tremulous tone,
Into something startling, and only known,
When those we worship, the loving and good,
Are stricken by death in their womanhood.

Still the months go by and the slow years fade
Into memories sad, and the darkest shade
Of a passionless longing seems to lie
In the lustreless depths of her mild blue eye,
And the hue of her cheek, so pure and pale,
Seemeth to one like a delicate veil

Revealing the rivulet veins where flows
The languishing blood, that comes and goes
With each dull throb of the suffering heart,
That flutters and trembles, with sudden start,
When falling leaves, or the wind, or the rain,
Or a song he loved bringeth once again
To her desolate life a golden gleam
Of the joys that died with her girlhood's dream.

The loved ones watch, with a mute despair,
As she grows each day more frail and fair,
And weep when their thoughts can only trace,
In the deep'ning lines of her wistful face,
Implora pace, a wearisome prayer—
While the hectic flush, that is mant'ling there,
Seems telling the tale of her life's great wrong,
And shadowing forth the hast'ning doom
Of her heart's best hope.
Through the gath'ring gloom

Of the drearisome days, so lonely and long,
  She sits with her woe in a cheerful room,
Singing a snatch of a sorrowful song,
  Or dreaming of rest in the quiet tomb.

———o———

From the saddest of all sad things of life,
  A weary woman wasting away,
Let us turn to the City's ceaseless strife,
  And note the progress of Reuben Grey.

Aug. Hoppin

V.

BUSINESS AND FLIRTATION.

Where "Co." in gilt letters over the door
Of a marble-veneered Broadway store
Is his simple alias, we find him still
Making his mark, as a young man will
  Gotten up for public inspection ;
Where luxury, with a thousand charms,
  Disguises Trade's deception,
And avarice, with rapacious arms,
  Extends a glad reception
To those whose arrogant family name
Is bruited abroad, on the breath of fame,

As having the clearest kind of a claim
  To its avenue reputation ;
Or those who wander, by twos and fours,
Doing a hundred different "chores"
(It never rains, you know, but it pours)
For country friends, and enter the stores
  For the purpose of permutation ;
Where many a sturdy and stalwart clerk,
With a fawning and flippant smile and smirk,
Is doing the lightest of feminine work,
  And filling a woman's station,
  Believing it man's vocation
To stand all day, in a Beau Nash shape,
Measuring satin and silk and tape
  For ladies whose aspiration
  Oft causes the aberration
Of lovers and husbands, whose cankering care
Is to furnish for them that exceedingly rare
Nondescript known as something to wear,

Never yet worn by a single fair
  One of our dressy American nation.
  This rock, many claim, any man may shun ;
But we offer a query or two for replies
  (A subterfuge for this long digression):
How is it when a man evinces surprise,
On beholding its very portentous size,
And, fearing a shipwreck, earnestly tries
To avoid the spot where the danger lies?
Doesn't the dear creature, from lips and eyes,
  With the force of an Arab's flying barb, or
Any fierce thing you're pleased to name,
Volley the feelings which happen to rise,
In urging her wardrobe's weighty claim,
Till the poor man, so persistently prest,
Seems like an impotent "Star of the West"
  In a bellipotent Charleston harbor?
Does the firing cease till the ensign comes
Down by the run, and he calmly succumbs,

Surrendering, against his intention,
A cargo of dresses and laces, velvets and rings,
Mantillas and muslins, embroideries and gloves,
Boots, brooches and bonnets, nuncupated "sweet
loves,"
With a host of mysterious, though wearable things,
Too numerous even to mention?

———o———

Said Hi-chwo-ki, the nomadic green tea drinker,
Kneeling to Haroun Al Raschid the Bland,
With Chi-Chille Blue, the famous Lapland tinker,
At the side of Zaman, the Syrian thinker,
Surrounded by dancers from Samarcand,
In the Royal Palace of Ispahan
(*Vide* Stoddard's curious arabesque plan
Of the paradisaical pagan land):
He said, says he, "The orientals learn
Every man to freeze to his own Tea-Urn."

The aphorism's a wise one (albeit chwo-ki
His own epitaph made when he said it),
So we'll give digression hereafter the go-by,
And the tea-drinker honor and credit.

Merely turning aside, for the nonce, to suggest
To Miss Flora Mac Flimsey, of Madison square,
And her host of dear friends who've nothing to wear,
That the lovers and husbands, who give you no rest
For the fault that they find when you wish to invest
A few thousand dollars in elegant clothes,
Are the first to look sour and turn up the nose
If you're not at all hours exquisitely dressed,
Which fact friend Butler, in "Nothing to Wear,"
Doesn't mention,
And as every one knows

With strange inattention;
To his readers' desires and moderate wishes
To know, to a plate, the number of dishes
It takes to go round at the family meal
Of his friends, the Mac Flimseys, of Madison square,
Through the whole of his rhyming forgets to reveal
The existence of Carrie, a sister of Flora's,
Who numbers our Reuben among her adorers.

Now Reuben has heard of the bonds and stocks,
The twenty per-cents.
And corpulent rents
Accruing from lands and colossal blocks
In old Mac Flimsey's possession;
And as old Mac's gout,
With the paralytic and deathly shocks,
Occurring in quick succession,

Would send him soon, he hadn't a doubt,
On the journey slow every one must go,
To the city where, ranged in a solemn row,
The "houses are all alike you know,"
To answer a query proposed by himself,
Thinking little of Carrie and much of the pelf,
Figured awhile and was pleasantly shown,
By bringing this "rule of three" into play,
The Parson, : sweet Carrie, : : and Reuben Grey,
That a very slight thing might make them his own.

Flora, you know, didn't go to the ball;
Carrie did! and as every one knew
On the whole avenue,
And reported next day, that the cost of her shawl
With the rest of her get-up was not a dime less
Than a great many thousands; were forced to confess,
In tones slightly hinting of worm-wood and gall,

That the grouping of colors was really quite new,
While the richness, uniqueness and set of her
dress,
With her stylish appearance, had started them all
On a race for new laurels:
'Twas Carrie's grand come-out, in fact her *debut,*
And how to describe her?
Now could we but bribe her,
With a set of rich corals,
A black-and-tan terrier with delicate feet,
A white Japanese fan, or an opera seat,
To give her consent to a full-page view
Of her latest and most impressive *visite,*
The description were nearly completed;
But we hav'n't a doubt she would plainly say,
She intends to be taken, some pleasant day—
To be cut, however, is hardly the way
A young lady expects to be treated!
But to give an idea of her presence that night,

Aside from all frivolous punning,
We quote Flashy Fitznoodle's as very near right,
It was "overwhelmingly stunning;"
And speaking of "dress" he said with a drawl,
"'Twas tangibly plain she outstripped them all."

As she entered the hall in her gorgeous pride,
Her dazzling diamonds increasing the light,
And the hearts of the envious fretting,
To a cynic we said, in a stage-aside,
"Such a classical head is of course supplied
With an intellect worthy the setting."
"Intellect! brains!!" he sneeringly said,
Manifesting an obdurate passion;
"Brains, my dear boy, in such a picturesque head,
Is at present an obsolete fashion."
So we found, for we stood in a neighb'ring set
Through the whole of the drearisome Lancers,
Heard her partner's questions, and tried to forget,

But remembered her wearisome answers,
And some of the feminine speeches she made,
Within hearing of many grave dancers:
She "had seen such a heavenly white Brocade,"
"Abhorred those detestable Moirés,"
"Found Stewart's a delectable place to trade,"
And "hated such odious soirées;"
"Had been frightened to death by hideous mice,"
"The Stuckups were horrible creatures,"
"Perfectly idolized Smith," "thought Shakespeare nice,"
"And adored the Trinity Preachers;"
And so forth, and so on, for an hour or two more,
In interims of flirting and dancing,
'Till, hungry and faint she sailed through the door,
With Reuben in tow, in search of that more
Tangible pleasure by few called a bore,
By Miss Carrie "superbly entrancing."

We followed soon after and found her engaged,
At the head of a sumptuous board,
Appeasing her hunger, a trifle enraged
At a party, who'd pompously poured
Out the chocolate, and, in passing her chair,
Chanced to sneeze, which suddenly floored
The whole of his stock, hot choc'late, saucer and cup;
"Illustrative," Carrie was loud to declare,
"Of the way Fussy Stuckup's waiters were bred,"
When, suddenly turning her arrogant head,
She found
Within sound
Of all she had whispered and sneeringly said,
The irate and unfortunate elderly Stuckup;—
Who, with bowings profound,
Nearly down to the ground,
Acknowledged the honor, and then turning red—

Turned sharp on his heel,
Leaving Carrie her shame and chagrin to conceal
As she could, which she did by preparing
A fresh plate of salad, while Reuben, despairing
Of a word or a gesture or even a glance
Till supper was finished,
Reconnoitered the tables to see if a chance
Were left him to furnish her palate and eyes
With the *cuisine's* latest and crowning surprise,
Which he found, with celery nearly embowered,
—Secreted for fear of its being devoured—
Then, giving Grant's strategy fullest observance,
Succeeded in flanking some five or six servants,
And retreating in safety—the edible prize
Surrendered to Carrie, when its esculent size
Was quickly diminished:

On receiving soon after the tenantless dish,
Reuben started as if he'd been shot ;

For expecting her thanks, an irascible wish
For something to eat, she didn't care what,
Was all that he got.
"She was starving to death, and there on the spot
Could devour every ration
Sent to the army;" Then, deploring his lot,
Reuben, weary and hot,
With a heavy sensation
Of having his hands full, rallied his forces,
And ordered the waiters to hurry the courses,
Vociferously issued a mandate beside,
To each contraband vassal, to have her supplied
In the shortest possible space of time,
And style sublime,
With ample dishes of fowl and meat,
And gustable spices,
Pickles and sauces and creams and game,
And delicate slices

Of various things 'twere hard to name,
With ornate devices
In jellies and ices,
Concocted by Taylor at fabulous prices—
And in short, whatever, acrid or sweet,
Stuckup had furnished the party to eat.

With as stately an air and as solemn a face
As ever you'd wish to see,
Each ebony F. F. V.
Took the orders below and returned to his place,
In time for the grand *entreé,*—
When with dignified mien, and a measured pace,
A dozen at least we'll say,
(As Hoppin doth show
In his etching you know),
Marched down the saloon, and established a base
Of lavish supplies just back of the chair
Of Carrie Mac F., of Madison square,

Where, gazing with awe and wondering at her,
  Each waiting a chance to deposit a plate,
Dish, or tureen or a well loaded platter,
  That Reuben had ordered, allow us to state
We left them, the supper, the crowd and the ball,
Struck palms with the Stuckups, then passed
    through the hall
And the doorway, down the front steps through
    the yard,
  And thought, as we finally stood in the street,
That Reuben was playing an excellent card,
  In furnishing Carrie with plenty to eat.

Which judgment was found to be very near right,
For, after the supper at Stuckups that night,
She took, it was said, a peculiar delight
    In his slightest word or attention;
And for many weeks after, to and fro,
Wherever she happened to come or go,

At her whim's suggestion, Reuben, we know,
Was willingly led, nor once did he show
    Resistance or even dissension.
At dinners and bouts, promenades and reviews,
Parades and ovations, receptions and balls,
Concerts and parties, and fashionable calls,
Late afternoon drives on the grand avenues,
And somnolent hours in the Trinity pews,
At operas whenever sonorous Donzatti
Quavered in basso for mellifluous Ad. Patti,
Riding or walking, on the Square or Broadway,
At home or abroad, at the church or the play,
And with truth, in a very emphatic way,
        We may say,
    Wherever she shone resplendent
He was found at her side, in his best array,
    Her most attentive attendant.

Confidentially then by many 'twas bruited,

And whispered about that Miss Carrie was suited
With Reuben, and of course he was dying for
Carrie;
Then the rumor and story, which rapidly spread,
That she'd ordered rich dresses and things for
her head
From a Parisian firm, and would very soon marry
Her reverent lover;
The invidious smiled, and maliciously said
It wasn't the lady he was going to wed,
As she would discover,
Ere three months were over,
Or the honeymoon fled,
But her portion of old Mac's lucre instead.

VI.

FINANCIAL RUIN WITH A LIGHT AHEAD.

While Reuben was sporting his avenue airs,
Cheatum, Fibit & Co.'s financial affairs,
Through the failure of Southern firms and trade,
    Indorsements and loans, with various
Fancy investments delusively made,
By advice of the ravenous Wall street bears,
(Not to mention deposits with Catchem & Co.)
        Had come to know,
        As their books would show,
    A position quite precarious,—
Which fact was announced one dubious day

By the serious seniors, who had their say,
Regarding his gay
Extravagant way
Of disbursing the greenbacks and giving the go-by
To the problem of getting them, to which no reply
By Reuben was made, though he very well knew
He must shorten his sail,
Or shipwreck and ruin would swiftly ensue,
While the firm, by the gale
Blowing 'mid breakers and brokers, would glide
From moorings on 'change down bankruptcy's tide!
But, consoling himself, he sagaciously said,
On the waters abroad he was casting his bread,
With assurances full, of returns forty-fold,
In position and gold,
When the world should behold

In his bride,
The heiress and pride
Of the house of Mac Flimsey, of Madison square,
To the which, he bethought him, that night he'd repair,
And an end put at once to all doubts and surmises
Concerning his future, then and there to declare
Eternal devotion, when the richest of prizes
Would be his by possession,—
For 'twas Reuben's impression
The vaguest of hints at a thought or intention
Of presenting his hand, and Carrie would mention
Wedded life and its joys, the day, hour and minute
When her wardrobe and self would be to begin it
In readiness waiting,
Which, after debating,

He trusted and hoped would be soon, for the day
On which she would say
To the world and himself, in a prominent way,
Thenceforth he alone was her lord and her mas-
ter,
Would see him insured from financial disaster.

The day went its way, as was often the practice
With well-behaved days whose existence was
cast
In years that are past,
And as often the case was and frequent the fact is
Regarding most nights, the night came at last;
When Reuben, still sanguine, and confident still
Of fullest success, went to work with a will,
And got himself up in a manner to kill
All sharp criticism concerning his dress,
Embellished the thoughts he intended to press
Upon Carrie Mac F. to prompt her to bless

His drearisome life as soon as she could;
Slowly footed the streets, instead of the bill
For carriage or 'bus, and finally stood
Quite anxious to cross over threshold and sill,
On the marble steps, at the rosewood door
Of the elegant mansion number four-
Teen hundred and something Madison square,
Which, (to himself, he was led to declare,
As over the structure from basement to garret
He rapidly glanced,) he expected to share,
And wasn't afraid anywhere to declare it;
Being elated, as you can see,
By writing down Carrie
As anxious to marry
Prognosticating the "yet-to-be,"
And thinking Mac Flimsey early intended
To finish his race for position and riches,
And leave to the youngest the grandest of niches
Known in the city; which monologue ended,

Mac FLIMSEY
BOBBETT-HOOPER SC
Hoppin

Suddenly, then, by the summoned appearance
Of the quintessence of blackness, which, with a
grin,
And obsequious "Sarvant, Sah," ushered him in,
Took charge of his hat, and gave him a clear-
ance
Into the parlors set apart
To the cabinet-maker's elaborate art,
Where nervously watching, in silence alone,
The drawing-room door
Thirty minutes or more,
He expectantly sat, then pacing the floor,
Till it seemed to his brain, a week—
(To speak
Within bounds) had leisurely flown,
Since he'd uttered a word, or heard the tone
Of familiar voices echo his own.

Then, for merest amusement, audaciously tore

A spotless fly-leaf from a volume found,
With leaves uncut, though attractively bound,
Upon which he inscribed each infliction and bore
On young men imposed without reason or cause,
Filled both pages full ere he came to a pause,
(Which paper was picked up next morning and
read
At the table by Flora, who spitefully said:
"The author 'mong Southerners must have been
bred,"
She noticed, which fact to his shame is confest,
That "*Waiting for Young Ladies*" led all the
rest.)

Still the lady came not, while the minutes, slow
And somniferous, seemed reluctant to go,
And lingered and lengthened each separate beat,
Till Reuben impatient resolved to retreat
From the house to the street,

But thinking it over, ere leaving his seat,
Reversed his decision, and wisely declined
To vote himself blind,
Or vacate the room, for thereby his chances
To help and improve his failing finances
Would be lessened, he thought,
So he did as he ought,
Kept his seat and his temper, and patiently sought
To keep his eyes open by gazing at pictures
And paintings, statuettes and things that are brought
From Florence or Rome, and recklessly bought
(By fashionable buyers who "go it blind"),
Subject to critical strictures;
When, just as he'd made up his mind
That he had become
Decidedly dumb,
And one of the permanent fixtures,
Miss Carrie appeared

In her most bewitching at-home-you-know style,
Gave Reuben her hand and then, with a smile,
Protested and feared
She was not over-stating
The truth when she said,
He was weary waiting,
So slowly had fled
The drearisome moments he'd passed there alone,
Quite lonesome, indeed, he must have grown,
And other things in a tender tone
That wakèd his hope like a rose new blown
All trouble compensating.
He saw fruition of all his hope,
As bright as a bubble blown from soap;
He saw a vista before him ope
That led to scenes resplendent,
Where, with Carrie, his beautiful bride,
He roamed forever 'mid airs of pride,
Or drifted along on fortune's tide

Without an ill attendant.
So bright the vision seemed to be
That in a moment of ecstasy
Upon the bones of his dexter knee
He incontinently dropped,
Then spoke the piece he'd learnt by heart,
How love had made his bosom smart,
How she could heal it by her art,
How would she have him, till death should part,
And the question was duly "popped."
No reply was made,
Could she be afraid
At the ardent fervor his words displayed?
Was she thinking just how to accept the ring?
Could she trembling be
In young love's tender agony,
Overcome by his manner of doing the thing?
He looked in her eyes to read his lot,
They were cold and blue like minie shot,

And didn't suggest the "forget-me-not,"
For they gazed at him derisively,
Then tossing her head
She cuttingly said
"I'm *engaged,* sir!" most decisively.

Had a guerrilla appeared in her place,
With a sardonic leer on its hideous face,
His surprise would have been decidedly less
Than it was when he heard her coolly confess,
That not for a moment in all of her life
Had she harbored a thought of being his wife.
She was shocked, indignant at what he had
said,
He couldn't consider her decently bred
If he thought she would wed
A man with less than ten thousand a year;
Then as turning away
Paused merely to say,

With her voice provokingly loud and clear,
" We're strangers hereafter, you know, Mr. Grey!"

He heard and saw her glide over the floor
Out of his sight through the drawing-room door,
Sealing at once and forever his doom;
When of a sudden, with irate mien,
Mac Flimsey the elder was plainly seen
Bearing hurriedly down from a distant room;
He didn't salute him as oft he had
When, (at the thought of marrying,
His hopes and his heart were bright and glad—)
With "Mr. Mac Flimsey, is Carrie in?"
For a something that gleamed in the father's eye
Put the thought in his head that he'd better keep shy
And a veto on longer tarrying.

So Reuben departed in great disgust
And brushed from off his feet the dust,
And vowed no more in signs to trust,
And railed at Fortune as all unjust!—
He didn't feel so much the snub,
  As loss of the cash he hoped to win,
  How could he manage to raise the "tin"
And save his firm? Ah, there was the rub,
And happening then to pass the "Club"
  Despairingly ventured in.

And there they were a roystering crew,
Who played and drank as most clubs do,
And lost their money and reason too,
While time on crazy pinions flew,
When Reuben thought he'd venture "a few"
  On the giddy wheel there turning;
He played and lost with a fevered brain—
He played and lost and lost again,

Playing with expectation vain,
  The lamp of hope still burning,
Till, with the force of fortune's spite,
The lamp went out—and all was night!

The gayest buck on the bright Broadway
Was the whilom rural Reuben Grey—
A desperate game he had to play,
    And, as many said, he "went it."
No millionaire of the bullion mart
'Ere acted so well his given part—
It seemed he'd the money-coining art,
    So lavishly he spent it.
He threw the gold dust left and right,
Until he quite obscured the sight
Of creditors regarded bright,
    Of Messrs. Cheatum & Fibit;
They saw the glitter and outside show,
But nothing at all of the undertow

That bore them on to the rocks below
As fate might soon exhibit.

Now speculation ran very wild,
The wheels of the Stock Exchange were oiled
By oil wells far too many;
And some that with scarce a nickel begun,
Were millionaires by the set of a sun,
And some lost every penny.
And among the rest
That chanced to invest,
Were Cheatum, Fibit & Co., to wrest
Their fortunes from ruin that sorely prest,
When a turn of the wheel
Made their bark to reel,
And stranded her with a broken keel;
Published then in the bankrupt's place,
They sank to the depths of commercial disgrace;—
He would not the path of the past retrace

And Reuben's career was ended.
Farewell his early auriferous dream
When he started out on life's broad stream,
With sails all drawing and wind abeam,
And everything seemed splendid.
A sweet revenge for Percy Lee!
Could she his failing fortune see,
Her heart might now exult in glee,
Could love be thus capricious;
But true love always is the same,
Undimmed its sweet undying flame,
Surviving wrong and sin and shame,
And never yielding the once dear name,
However soiled or vicious.
Poor Reuben's summer-time friends were flown,
Not one left of the fawning crew;
None would now a friendship own
For one who hadn't a single sou.
They cut him openly in the street,

And he bitterly thought of the peaceful past,
And early friends, and that love so sweet,
Which like a dolt to the winds he'd cast;
But he hadn't arrived at the Prodigal pitch,
Nor brought himself to act as "sich"—
He couldn't go back without being rich.

Despair now seized on Reuben Grey,
With desolation round his way;
He drank, his misery to allay,
And, more degraded day by day—
All passed his former assumption;
He felt he had played a foolish part,
And steered by a false and erring chart,
That had wrecked on sunken rocks his heart,
And cursed his want of gumption.

VII.

MANHOOD VINDICATED.

War's lurid flame had fired the land—
The rebels' parricidal hand
  Was menacing the nation's heart,
When Lincoln's call, like a grand command,
  Was excitedly read in village and mart;
Full many a chivalrous sire and son
Seized eagerly then his sword or gun,
Gave short farewells to each dear one,
And marched with steady heart and true
  To the deadly front, to find a name

That would lustre shed on the scroll of fame;
Or, sadder, perchance, as they little knew,
A lonesome grave by the dank bayou.

From every mountain and every dale
Was heard the tramp of earnest men
Marching to conflict, while the timid, pale,
Gave but their prayers, a boon regarded then,
Invoking God's own blessing on the right,
To guard their loved ones in the perilous fight,
And bring them safely to their arms again.
And Freedom in the dust, with uplift hands,
Called loud for aid and was not denied;
For, as if stricken by Divine commands,
Its iron chains fell off, and Freedom, glorified,
Stood up in might, a power in all the land,
Majestical and grand.
And Reuben heard

The electric word,
And the latent manhood within him stirred.

Anon he stands,
A musket bright in his feeble hands,
Ready to die, if need be, and why live?
Since life had nothing for him to give,
But all the life and strength he had
His country claimed,
His wearied heart grew light and glad
That he was not named
Among the hopeless yet, that he might yet achieve
Something, retrieve something,
And die, and, thus dying, live.
'Twas thus he felt on an after day,
As he marched with his regiment down Broadway,
'Mid cheering crowds, who, with loud hurras,

Gave them God-speed as they marched to the
wars,
While ladies tearfully showered bouquets
On brave, true men bound off for the frays
Where many might fall, but on whose emprise
Hinged immortal destinies.

The flags were afloat on the summer air,
Waving their last benedictions there,
And a solemn triumph seemed to dwell
In the season; each one knew too well
The terrible truth, that many an one
Who marched that day with gleaming gun—
With prayerful face and heart a-calm
Would find a grave by a Southern palm.

With open ranks and hurried tread
They swept through the clamorous throng;
Reuben, busy with bright hopes fled,

Humming over an old time song—
Or wond'ring if Percy Lee would shed
A tear when the fearful list she read,
And knew of a truth that—he was dead,—
Suddenly turned to the left his head,
And a tableau saw that touched his pride
And quickened the flow of his heart's warm tide;
There in her carriage in queenly state,
Carrie Mac Flimsey, the haughty, sate,
Who gazed on the scene
With as icy a mien
As though it a holiday pageant had been;
While Flashy Fitznoodle,
Faced like a poodle,
Stood at her side, a thing of hate.
Their glances met in a cold calm way,
And not a line of her meaningless face
Gave the faintest hint that Reuben Grey
Had even held a respectable place

Among the many who used to grace
Her circle of friends;
Then thinking 'twould pay,
Fitz. managed to stand
With his hat in his hand—
And gave him a look, superciliously grand,
In which he undoubtedly wished to say
And have the poor private understand,
That the elegant lady there at his side,
Was, in prospective, his personal bride!
And the maddest and saddest man that day,
In the long blue ranks was Reuben Grey;
But the feeling gave way to a stern intent,
And a higher thought, as along he went.—
He had suffered much in adversity's school,
Had gathered some wisdom by being a fool,
And wished for a better story;
The field was broad his soul to try,
And now determined to do or die,

He scorned the scorn of Fitznoodle's eye,
    And marched along to glory.

Did he find it? say you; ask the plain,
Where the deadly bullets fell like rain,
Sweeping down rows of men like grain,
That never may rise to life again—
Where the wounded lay in bitter pain
Upon the heaps of peaceful slain,
That may never rise to battle again!
Foremost was he in the deadly fight,
His courage true, his spirit bright,
    And his life seemed one enchanted;
His voice was heard where the breath of strife,
Death's dread malaria, most was rife,
And he gave to the work his all of life—
    His energy undaunted.
And step by step he rose apace,
And ne'er did dignities justlier grace

One who had stood in the deadly place,
    And no tongue spoke detraction ;
Till, suddenly, as if his work were o'er,
And the cup of his life could hold no more,
    He fell in a desperate action.

VIII.

PERCY LEE.

Now, the war was felt at the village green,
For hard they struggled and toiled, I ween,
    To raise the "quota" required:
And meetings were held and the band was out,
And the boys of the village went drumming
        about,
    And the farmers' hearts were fired.
The women met in the church each day,
And worked for the brave boys far away—
Worked without any let or stint,
Tore up their sheets to make them lint,

Made them wrappers and woolen socks,
And queer "housewives," and havelocks,
And things that never were understood,
Only that their intent was good;
And none displayed more energy
Than the beautiful, gentle Percy Lee.

Her heart long bowed with its hidden grief,
In relieving others, found relief;
  The dull home scenes monotonous grew,
    And slowly the long months wore away,
  While the weary world was full, she knew,
    Of sorrow and pain she might allay;
So with long farewells in a trembling tone,
  And the Parson's blessing, (who thinks of the day,
  Of his farewell blessings on Reuben Grey,)
She went from the scenes her youth had known
  Into the strange wide world alone.

* * * * * * *

In the hospital ward, with a heavy heart,
  But wearing a smile on her patient face,
A gentle woman performs a part
  That gives to mercy a sweeter grace.

Full many a time when the pale lips stirred,
  At the closing up of some terrible day,
Hath she bowed her head for a tender word,
  To send to the dear ones far away.

And many a brave boy dying near,
  Feebly calling as best he could,
The sweet fond name of one most dear—
  Thought at his side the loved one stood.

The dying groan and the failing breath,
  Startle the strongest ears to hear,
But still she moves 'mid pain and death,
  Breathing blest words of hope and cheer.

Through desolate nights and wearisome days
She thoughtfully watches, and tenderly prays
Over many a wounded one, who lies
With feverish breath and closèd eyes ;

But each day bringeth its own reward,
    For, moving among the wounded there,
Their heartiest thanks they oft accord
    In strong rough words of praise and prayer.

As there she moved on her mission of love,
    After a terrible battle was done,
Speaking sweet words of comfort and cheer,
    To many a ghastly and stricken one ;
A moaning voice saluted her ear,
That all the blood in her heart did move ;
She trembling stood, nor dared to look
    At the wounded officer laying near,
Till again the voice her being shook,

Recalling of life the love so dear—
Its memories haunting her even here.

There wounded, senseless and dying lay
The love of her youth—her Reuben Grey.
Her's now alone, unconscious, but dear—
More dear than when, in that far off year,
She parted from him with prayer and tear!
And oh! how she watched his fluttering breath,
As if 'twere presage of approaching death;
How she watched and longed for one blest ray
Of reason to lighten her life's dark day,
One glance of love that should compensate
For all of her ill at the hands of fate!

Oh! the long and the drear eclipse,
With not one star amid the gloom!
While the meaningless words from his fevered lips
Gave for her ardent hope no room;

Save when from the raving chaos came,
  As we hear in a storm the song of a bird—
A resemblance faint to the watcher's name,
  And old time memories faintly heard.
So Percy watched and worked and prayed,
  Till weary days and weeks had flown;
The long intreated boon delayed,
  She wept and waited—and that alone.

* * * * * * *

There came a change,
Sudden and strange,
As if in answer to all her prayer;
The loved eyes oped,
Had she had hoped,
With conciousness reflected there,
And gazed upon her radiant face,
Embodied excellence and grace;
And with a voice

That made rejoice
Her heart, he said:
"Pray tell to me
Are you an angel sent from heaven,
Or are you Percy Lee?"

———o———

No circumstance there is that tends
So much for wrong to make amends,
And such complete enjoyment lends,
As reconciling sundered friends;
And Reuben Grey and Percy Lee,
Were happy as they well could be;
Too wise by far to die was he,
Too loving far to let him she,
And all the sum of shame and doubt
From their account was blotted out.

IX.

A SLIGHT CHANGE.

Let us go back to the city again,
That great workshop of muscle and brain,
Where people sell themselves amain,
Assuming burdens of care and pain,
That they may the goal of "position" attain,
    Indulging in many a whimsey;
There came a choke in gold one day,
And stocks went down in a ruinous way.
    The "buyer's option" wouldn't hold,
    And "sellers short" were short in gold,
And borrowers failed and couldn't pay,
    And down went old Mac Flimsey!
A furniture auction at number four-

Teen hundred and something, Madison square,
Finished the whole, leaving nothing more
    Than the family coat-of-arms to spare.
        They moved at night,
        Disappeared from sight,
And no more walked in walks polite;
Fitznoodle, the poodle, cut them quite,
    And Flora fair and Carrie
Were left on hand, an unsaleable stock,
And no one sought their humble "block,"
    To make an offer to marry;
Mac Flimsey never is known to swear—
    But gets decidedly mad
Whenever he thinks of his daughters fair
    And the "chances" both have had,
And often, while moving away his chair
    From his meals, when things look bad,
Irascibly stops, aloud to declare
That, for *him*, such a bull is hard to bear.

X.

SETTLED.

Bells on the stilly morning air
    Wake the folk by the village green,
Richmond's fallen! they loud declare—
    The day long looked for now is seen,—
        And all rush out,
        With song and shout,
  And gather in crowds the church about;
And prouder than any on that glad day
Is the brave but feeble Reuben Grey,
Thinking of many a desperate fray—

The hospital ward, where he dying lay—
The peaceful scenes of his early years—
His city life of deceit and fears,
    And all the terrible after-strife
    For a purer heart and a better life :
His victory's won ! and the war is o'er,
  Peace has come, and rest for the weary band
Of volunteers ; and forever more
  The North and the South united shall stand,
  Defying the foes of Freedom's own land :
        While the Palm and the Pine
        In peace shall entwine
    Their branches as never before.

    Reuben feels in his heart
    That his humble part
      Was done on his "level best,"
    And limps about with an honest pride,
      A splintered arm on his breast,—

Saluting his friends on either side
And leaning (as we should say),
In a very unsoldierly way,
On Percy Lee's arm, "at rest."

———o———

A wedding occurred by the village green,
When the spring grew warm and bright,
And a fairer couple never was seen
Than greeted the people's sight,
As there in the village church they stood,
Where had assembled a multitude
Of simple people, in kindly mood,
To view the scene of calm delight.
And the village quidnuncs, one and all,
Could easy the day and hour recall
When they predicted Reuben would be
The dearest of all to Percy Lee.

* * * * * * *

Down to the village again if you will—
Drive a mile or so out from Adder Hill,
Then turn to the right, where a wild hurra
From a contraband brought home from the war
Will astonish your horse; and there, without
doubt,
If this happens at dusk, and they haven't gone
out,—
Under the porch where the shadows play,
Enjoying themselves in a rational way,
You will find "Mr. and Mrs. Colonel Grey."

* * * * * * *

Reuben finds a charm
On the old home farm,
That fills his life with a perfect joy.
With no wish to roam
From his humble home,
And pure and free from the world's alloy,

He lives as he lived when a careless boy,
    And mourns not wealth's denial;
A fearful ordeal his soul has passed,
Now safe, thank Heaven and Percy, at last;
He shudders as back his eyes are cast,
But feels like a tree that has braved the blast,
    The stronger for the trial.

www.ingramcontent.com/pod-product-compliance
Lightning Source LLC
LaVergne TN
LVHW021421110826
845150LV00007B/2023

9781425508692